ET

STORMS

Mark Maslin

RESTLESS PLANET

STORMS

Other titles in this series:

EARTHQUAKES FLOODS VOLCANOES

Cover photograph: A tornado strikes a town in Texas, USA, in the spring of 1995.

Title page: A tornado emerges from a spectacular storm cloud in the Midwest of the USA.

Contents page: The 'eye' of Hurricane Linda approaches Mexico in 1997.

First published in 1999 by Wayland Publishers Ltd,
61 Western Road, Hove, East Sussex, BN3 1JD, England
www. wayland.co.uk

This paperback edition published in 2000.

© Copyright 1999 Wayland Publishers Ltd

Consultant: Bill Clarke, Education Officer, The Natural
History Museum
Editor: Alison Cooper
Series editor: Polly Goodman, Philippa Smith & Nicola Wright
Series design: Stonecastle Graphics
Book design: Tim Mayer

British Library Cataloguing in Publication Data
Maslin, Mark
Storms. – (Restless Planet)
1. Storms – Juvenile literature
I.Title
551.5'5

ISBN 0 7502 2740 0

Printed and bound by G.Canale & C.S.p.A, Turin

Acknowledgements
The publishers would like to thank: Associated Press 4/Dave
Martin, 12/Victor R. Caivano, 19/Topi Lyambila, 23/Stefano
Sarti, 44/ Dario Lopez Mills; Camera Press 20/Kelly Kerr &
Newsmakers, 36/Newsmakers, 38/Vienna Report, 39/Vienna
Report, 43 (bottom)/Benoit Gysembergh; Robert Harding
6/Schuster; Impact 17/Javeed A. Jafferji, 43 (top)/Mark Cator;
Oxford Scientific Films/Warren Faidley *title page*, 15, 28;
Popperfoto/AFP 35/Yuri Cortez; Popperfoto/Reuters 11/Rick
Wilking, 22/Shaun Best, 24/Rafiqur Rahmann, 32/Juan Carlos
Ulate; Rex Features 31/Sipa Press, 34; Science Photo Library
contents page/NASA & Goddard Space Flight Center, 5/
Gordon Garrard, 26/David Ducros, 27 (both)/David Parker,
29/NASA & Goddard Space Flight Center; Tony Stone Images
Cover; 16/Paul Sonders, 25/H. Richard Johnston; Topham 30.

All artwork is by Tim Mayer, except pages 18/Nick Hawken;
13/Tony Townsend; 6, 8 (top), 17 (lower), 21/Wayland
Picture Library.

Contents

HURRICANE WREAKS HAVOC

Hurricane Georges yesterday unleashed ferocious winds, torrential rain and flooding on the states bordering the Gulf of Mexico as thousands of people were evacuated. 'The wind is really blowing out there and things are hitting the windows,' said Rachel Alonso from a shelter in Gulfport, Mississippi... At least 320 people were killed by the hurricane last week when it lashed the Caribbean and the Florida Keys. Hundreds of thousands were made homeless.

Adapted from *The Guardian*, 29 September 1998

Imagine being caught in a hurricane. Winds are roaring around you at speeds of over 300 kph. It takes 500 trillion horsepower to whirl these winds at such tremendous speeds – that's enough power to meet the USA's energy needs for a hundred years. Could you survive such a storm? Perhaps...

If you were caught out in the open you might survive by climbing into a ditch or even by lying flat on the ground. This would reduce the chance of the wind picking you up and throwing you around in the air. If you were at home the safest place to shelter would be the cellar.

▼ Three men struggle through the storm waves in 90 mph winds on 25 September 1998, as Hurricane Georges struck Florida Keys, in the USA.

Nowhere on the planet's surface is safe from the effects of storms. Blizzards pound northern Europe, Asia and America, while hurricanes hurtle across the tropical oceans and tornadoes spin violently over the continents. A major storm can cause devastation across several countries, although most storms have much less serious effects. This book explains how storms are caused, where they occur, the damage they can inflict and what scientists can do to try to predict them.

▲ Fork lightning over the town of Tamworth, in New South Wales, Australia during a storm.

What Causes Storms?

Storms occur all over the world, but certain types of storm are much more common in some areas than others. Winter blizzards, for example, are quite common in the far north of Europe, but very unusual in the countries around the Mediterranean Sea. This is because storms are linked to different climates around the world, and so to understand what causes storms you first need to find out more about climate.

Hot and cold Earth

The different climates on our planet are caused by the middle of the Earth – the Equator – receiving more of the Sun's heat than the Poles. At the Equator the Sun is directly overhead and it is here that the Earth receives the most heat. As you move north or south from the Equator, the surface of the Earth curves away from the Sun. The Sun's heat is spread over a larger area, and thus warms the Earth less. At the Poles, the Sun's heat is spread out so much that the Arctic and Antarctic are extremely cold all year round.

▲ Ice and snow cover Antarctica all year round.

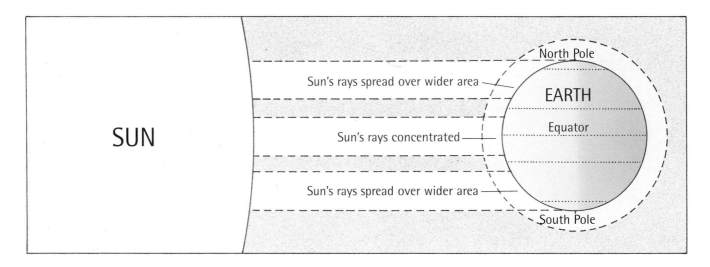

SUN

Sun's rays spread over wider area

North Pole

EARTH

Equator

Sun's rays concentrated

Sun's rays spread over wider area

South Pole

▲ This diagram shows how different parts of the Earth receive different amounts of energy from the Sun.

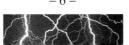

The white snow and ice of the Arctic and Antarctic are also very reflective surfaces. They bounce a lot of the Sun's heat back into space. The leafy green rain forests at the Equator are much less reflective, so this region absorbs a lot more energy. These two processes working together mean that the Equator is hot and the Poles are very cold. The difference in heat produces moving currents of air (wind) and water, which carry heat from the Equator to the Poles.

Spinning Earth

The movement of heat away from the Equator is affected by the spinning of the Earth. The rotation of the Earth causes air and ocean currents to be pushed (deflected) to the right (clockwise) in the northern hemisphere and to the left (anti-clockwise) in the southern hemisphere. This deflection is called the Coriolis force and its strength is greater at the Poles than at the Equator. An everyday example of the Coriolis force in action is the way water flows down a plughole. In the northern hemisphere water flows clockwise down the plughole, while in the southern hemisphere it flows anti-clockwise.

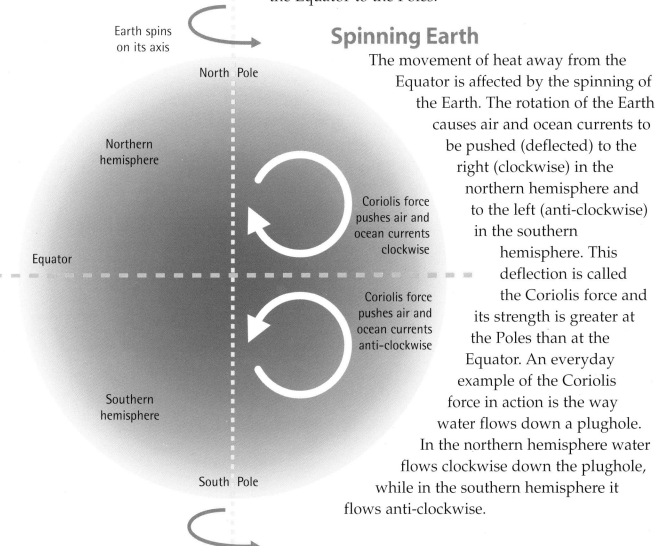

Earth spins on its axis

North Pole

Northern hemisphere

Coriolis force pushes air and ocean currents clockwise

Equator

Coriolis force pushes air and ocean currents anti-clockwise

Southern hemisphere

South Pole

▲ This diagram shows how the spin of the Earth on its axis affects the movement of air and ocean currents.

Global climate zones

Equatorial Lows

At the Equator the intense heat from the Sun warms the air. Warm air expands, and becomes less dense, so it rises. A space is created below it, and cooler air is sucked in to fill the space. This forms an area of low atmospheric pressure, which is known as the Equatorial Lows. The movement of air produces the Trade winds in both the northern and southern hemispheres.

Subtropical Highs

The hot tropical air which has risen high into the atmosphere slowly cools as it moves towards the Poles. At a latitude of about 30° it is cooler and denser than the surrounding air, so it sinks. This creates an area of high atmospheric pressure known as the Subtropical Highs. As the sinking air reaches the surface it spreads out. Air that moves towards the Equator becomes part of the Trade wind system, while the air that moves towards the Poles forms the Westerlies.

▼ This diagram shows how sinking and rising air creates areas of high and low pressure.

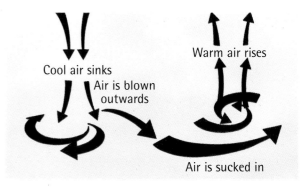

Cool air sinks

Air is blown outwards

Warm air rises

Air is sucked in

▲ High pressure at ground level

▲ Low pressure at ground level

▼ This map shows some of the major wind flows around the world. Winds are named after the direction they blow from. For example, Westerlies blow from the west.

Key

← Westerlies

← Trade winds

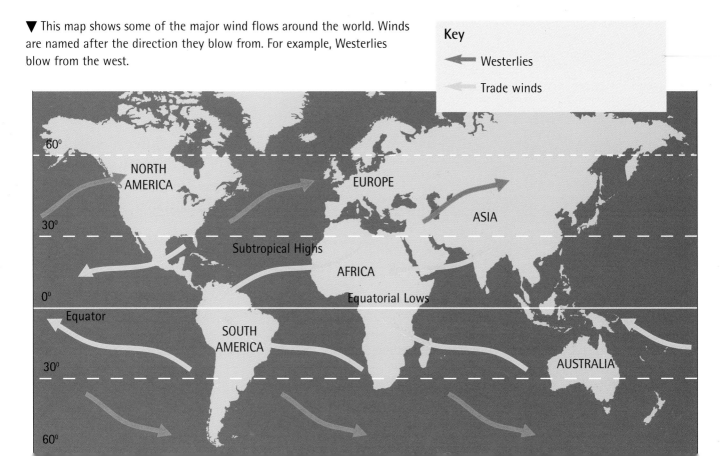

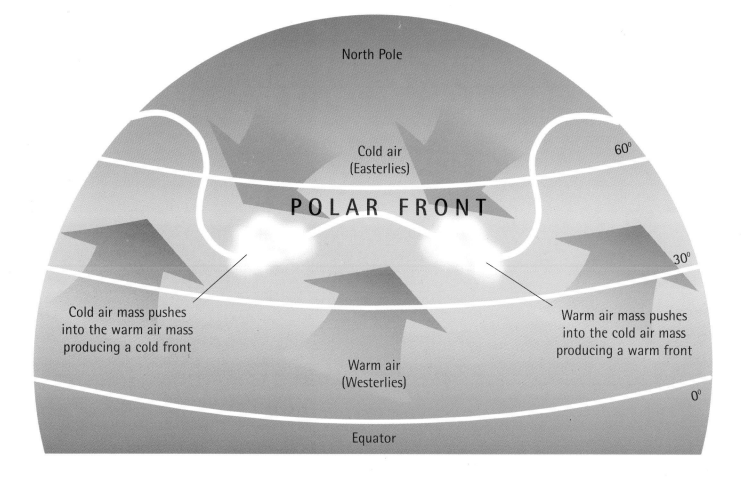

Labels in diagram:
North Pole

Cold air
(Easterlies)

60°

POLAR FRONT

30°

Cold air mass pushes
into the warm air mass
producing a cold front

Warm air mass pushes
into the cold air mass
producing a warm front

Warm air
(Westerlies)

0°

Equator

▲ This diagram shows how cold and warm air masses meet at the Polar Front.

Polar Front

There is also an area of high pressure at each of the Poles. This is because the intense cold causes air to become super-chilled and sink. Winds called Easterlies blow outwards from the high pressure area. Cold, polar air meets the warm, moist Westerlies at the Polar Front. The clash causes the Westerlies to lose a lot of their moisture in the form of rain.

Storm zones

Different types of storm occur in these different climate areas. The major storm zones are:

- the Polar Front, where cold, dry air meets warm, moist air. In the northern hemisphere, the Polar Front is over northern Europe and America during the winter, causing severe storms and blizzards.

- the Subtropical Highs and the Trade wind belt – these are where hurricanes begin (see pages 10–13).

Types of Storm

Hurricanes

Severe tropical storms that start in the North Atlantic Ocean, Caribbean Sea, Gulf of Mexico and north-east Pacific are called hurricanes. They are called typhoons in the western Pacific, and tropical cyclones in the Indian Ocean and Australasia. Hurricanes, typhoons and tropical cyclones are, however, all exactly the same type of storm and in this book they are all called hurricanes.

Hurricanes develop over the oceans and tend to lose their force once they move over land. They form in the tropics, where the Trade winds are sucked towards the Equator because of the hot air that is rising there (see pages 8–9). For a hurricane to begin to form, the sea temperature must be above 26 °C for at least 60 m below the surface and the air humidity must be about 75–80%. This combination provides the right amount of heat and water vapour to sustain the storm once it has started. A hurricane can form gradually over a few days, or in the space of just 6–12 hours.

▼ This map shows the main areas of the world that are affected by hurricanes.

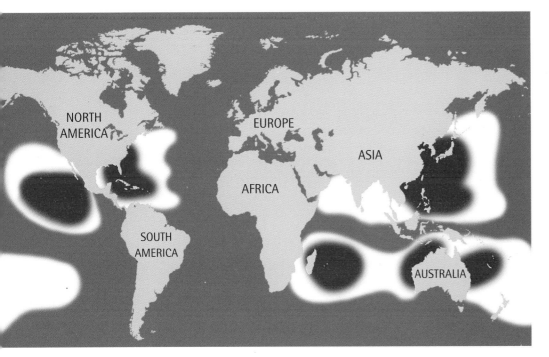

NORTH AMERICA

EUROPE

ASIA

AFRICA

SOUTH AMERICA

AUSTRALIA

Key

☐ Areas at risk from hurricanes

■ Main areas where hurricanes develop

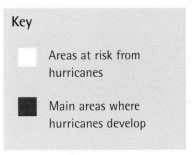

Hurricanes are rare

The conditions that are needed for a hurricane to form occur quite often, but it is quite rare for a hurricane actually to develop. There are a maximum of about 50 hurricanes a year. For a storm to be classified as a hurricane, the sustained wind speed must exceed 120 kph. In a fully developed hurricane, wind speeds can exceed 200 kph and its size can vary from 100 km to over 1,500 km. A hurricane will usually last for two or three days and then take about four to five days to die out.

▼ These people in Bermuda were putting boards over their windows to protect them from the winds of Hurricane Felix when they were hit by a huge storm wave, in August 1995.

CYCLONE HITS PAKISTAN

Up to 700 people are missing and feared drowned after a cyclone with wind speeds of 270 kph hit Pakistan's Arabian Sea coast. It caused tidal waves which flooded hundreds of fishing villages, and rescue efforts were delayed by lashing rain. 'People are saying entire villages are missing but the district administration is still trying to get there, so no one really knows,' said Dr Mumtaz Uqali.

Adapted from *Associated Press* report, 22 May 1999

How does a hurricane develop?

A hurricane begins to form when the warm ocean heats the air above it and the hot air rises. This produces an area of low pressure which sucks in the air around it. The hot, rising air contains a lot of water vapour that has evaporated from the surface of the ocean. As the air rises, it cools and cannot hold so much water vapour. Some of it condenses as water droplets and forms clouds. The transformation from water vapour to water droplets releases energy, called latent heat, which in turns warms the air even more. This makes it rise even higher. The air within a hurricane can rise to over 10,000 m above the ocean. This is the eye (centre) of the storm and the spiralling, rising air creates a huge column of cumulonimbus clouds.

▲ A house on the coast of Honduras is battered by storm waves and falling trees as Hurricane Mitch strikes on 28 October 1998.

When the air inside the hurricane cannot rise any higher, it flows outwards from the eye, producing a broad canopy of cirrus cloud. The air cools and falls back to sea-level, where it is sucked back into the centre of the storm. Because of the Coriolis force (see page 7), the air that is sucked into the bottom of a hurricane in the northern hemisphere spins into the storm in a clockwise direction, while the air escaping at the top spins out in an anti-clockwise direction.

The process works in the opposite direction in the southern hemisphere. (Remember the example of the water going down the plug hole.)

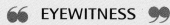

❝ EYEWITNESS ❞

"We were requested by a concerned family to bring an invalid man into the shelter. The rain squalls were still only occasional, so we ventured out. We went to a darkened house lit by a flashlight. Then the wind and rain became more ferocious and we quickly loaded the man on to the stretcher and rushed back to the shelter... The rain pelted us until we were drenched... Another family asked us to go out and pick up a relative but we could not due to the increased winds and rain. Some time after this the electricity failed and only the emergency lights stayed on. Those lights lasted maybe an hour and then they went out."

Paramedic George Metts recalls his experiences of the night Hurricane Hugo struck South Carolina in the USA, on 21 September 1989 (adapted from a report by the National Oceanic and Atmospheric Administration, USA).

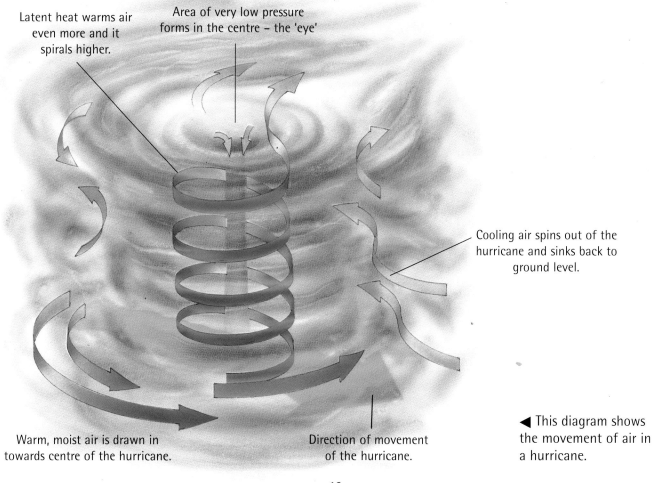

Latent heat warms air even more and it spirals higher.

Area of very low pressure forms in the centre – the 'eye'

Cooling air spins out of the hurricane and sinks back to ground level.

Warm, moist air is drawn in towards centre of the hurricane.

Direction of movement of the hurricane.

◀ This diagram shows the movement of air in a hurricane.

Tornadoes

A tornado is a violent, spinning column of air. From a distance, it looks like a cloud in the shape of an ice-cream cone. Tornadoes are most numerous and devastating in central, eastern and north-eastern USA, where an average of five per day are reported every May. They also occur in Australia (where there are around fifteen per year) and in the UK, Italy, Japan and Central Asia.

DID YOU KNOW?

Since 1925 tornadoes have killed 9,000 people in the USA – as many as the total number of people killed by floods (4,000) and hurricanes (5,000).

What causes tornadoes?

Tornadoes usually form over land rather than over tropical oceans, when there is warm, moist air near the ground and cold, dry air above it. These conditions occur frequently in late spring and early summer over the Great Plains of the USA. As the sun heats the ground, the warm, moist air rises. As it does so, it cools and forms large cumulonimbus clouds. The strength of the updraft produced by the rising air affects how much of the surrounding air is sucked into the bottom of the tornado.

Two things help the tornado to spin violently: the Coriolis force and the jet stream. As the jet stream passes over the top of the storm, it adds an extra twist to the tornado.

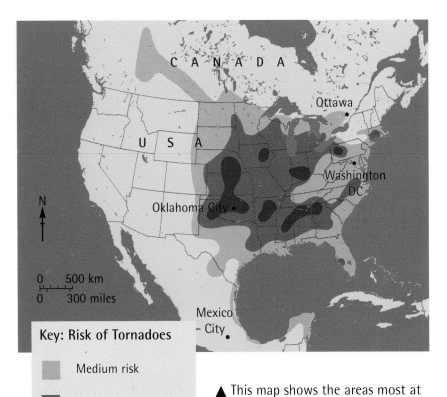

Key: Risk of Tornadoes

Medium risk

High risk

Highest risk

▲ This map shows the areas most at risk from tornadoes in North America.

66 EYEWITNESS 99

"I grabbed my dogs, shoved them into the bathroom, got the family into the tub and covered us with blankets. We just waited for the roof to peel off."

Linda Plunkett, survivor of the tornado that hit Oklahoma City, May 1999

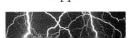

Measuring tornado strength

Two types of measurement are used to describe the strength of a tornado. The Fujita (F) Scale classifies the strength of a tornado according to the speed at which it rotates. This is important as it indicates how destructive the storm will be. Tornadoes classified as F1 are usually (but not always) harmless. F4 and F5 tornadoes are truly scary. However, on average there are only two F5 tornadoes per year in the USA, and they usually reach level 5 for just a few seconds. An F6 tornado is possible but no one has ever observed one.

The second type of measurement is called the Pearson Scale. This scale is used to measure the length and width of a tornado's path. Using these two scales, the potential damage and the area that is likely to be affected can be predicted.

▲ A tornado in the Midwest of the USA creates a swirling cloud of dust and debris.

FUJITA SCALE

Fujita scale	Rotation speed (kph)	Effects
F0 (weak)	Less than 116	Minor damage to buildings and trees.
F1 (weak)	117–180	Minor damage to buildings and trees.
F2 (strong)	181–253	Vehicles pushed off roads, roofs torn off buildings.
F3 (strong)	254–331	Vehicles lifted off ground, severe damage to weaker buildings, e.g.wooden houses.
F4 (violent)	332–418	Vehicles picked up and carried over 2 km, wooden and brick buildings destroyed.
F5 (violent)	419–512	Many buildings destroyed, depending on size of tornado.
F6 (extreme)	More than 512	Total devastation – nothing left standing.

▲ A mountaineer caught in a blizzard struggles to protect himself from the whirling snow.

DID YOU KNOW?

Hailstones form when water droplets high in the atmosphere become super-cooled to less than 0 °C and collide to form balls of ice. If you cut open a hailstone you can see the layers of ice that have built up – it looks a bit like the layers of an onion. Hailstones can vary in size from 2–200 mm.

Winter storms

Rain, ice, wind, hail and snow are common at the Polar Front and in high mountains, especially in the winter. The worst storms are called blizzards. These combine strong winds, ice, hail and driving snow. Temperatures can fall as low as -12 °C and you can see only a few metres in front of you.

At the Polar Front in the northern hemisphere, warm air from the subtropics pushing north-eastwards meets cold polar air trying to move south-west (see page 9). Waves develop at the point where the air masses meet and try to pass each other. This produces a warm front and a cold front. A similar process takes place in the southern hemisphere.

The warm, moist air is chilled and clouds develop. Rain, snow or hail may form, depending on how great the temperature difference is between the cold and warm air masses. For snow to reach the ground the temperature of the air between the clouds and the ground must be below 4 °C, otherwise the snowflakes melt as they fall.

Monsoons

Heavy rainstorms occur in the monsoon belt, which lies across southern Asia and parts of central Africa. In summer the land becomes very hot and the warm air over the land rises. An area of low pressure forms and sucks in air from the southern hemisphere. This air has travelled long distances over the oceans and is full of moisture. When the air passes over the land it has to rise. As it rises, it cools and releases moisture in the form of torrential rain – the monsoons.

These seasonal rains provide vital supplies of water in Asia and central Africa. About 40% of the world's population live in the monsoon belt and rely on the rains for drinking water, and for their crops and animals. Yet the rains can also cause catastrophic floods.

▲ Two boys on the island of Zanzibar in the Indian Ocean shelter from the monsoon rains.

◀ This map shows areas of the world affected by monsoons.

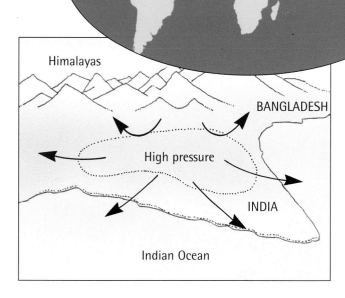

▲ 1. In winter, the land is cold. Dry, sinking air creates high pressure. Winds blow outwards.

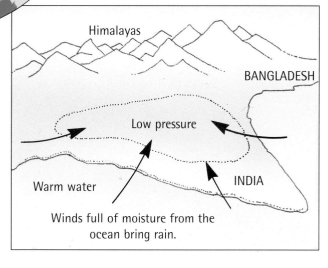

▲ 2. In summer the land heats up. Warm air rises, creating an area of low pressure. Warm, moist air is sucked in, bringing monsoon rains.

The El Niño Effect

Every few years an event takes place off the western coast of South America that has a dramatic effect on the world's weather. This event is known as El Niño, which is Spanish for 'The Boy Child', meaning Jesus, because it is often first noticed around Christmas time.

What is El Niño?

Normally, there is an area of low pressure over the western Pacific, where warm surface water heats the air above it. As the warm, moist air rises, more air is dragged across the Pacific and sucked in at sea-level. These strong air currents are the Trade winds. As they blow across the ocean they pull the surface water away from the coast of South America towards the centre of the Pacific. Colder water that is rich in nutrients wells up from deep in the ocean to replace it.

When El Niño occurs, the area of low pressure moves across into the centre of the Pacific Ocean, closer to South America. The Trade winds become weaker, the surface water is no longer dragged across the Pacific and the cold water almost stops rising from the ocean depths. The change in the flow of air across the ocean alters the direction of the jet stream, a narrow belt of strong winds high in the atmosphere. This brings stormy weather to areas far from the Pacific.

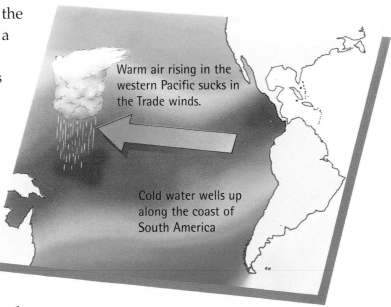

Warm air rising in the western Pacific sucks in the Trade winds.

Cold water wells up along the coast of South America

▲ 1 This diagram shows normal conditions in the Pacific Ocean.

The Trade winds become weaker. Warm surface water moves across to the centre of the Pacific Ocean.

Cold water almost stops rising to the surface

▲ 2 This diagram shows the changes caused by El Niño.

La Niña

Usually, the climate in the Pacific swings between normal conditions and warmer El Niño conditions. Occasionally, however, it swings the other way – from normal conditions to colder conditions. When this happens, the air in the western Pacific rises more strongly, the Trade winds become stronger too and much more cold water is dragged up from the deep ocean. These colder conditions are known as La Niña (Spanish for 'Little Girl'). You can think of El Niño and La Niña as being like the two ends of a seesaw, with normal conditions in the middle.

What effects does El Niño have?

By altering the position of air currents carrying moisture, El Niño can bring floods to some areas and droughts to others. The El Niño that occurred in 1982–3 was one of the strongest on record – some scientists think its after-effects can still be detected in the oceans. There were droughts and dust storms in Africa and Australia, while areas of Peru that normally receive only 250 mm of rain in a year were hit by 2 m of rain instead. El Niño is also thought to affect the way hurricanes develop and move across the Atlantic Ocean (see page 33).

▲ Parts of Kenya received unusually heavy rains in 1998. Many people believed that El Niño was responsible for disrupting normal weather patterns.

WHAT'S WRONG WITH OUR WEATHER?

Noah might have been impressed by the deluge that hit California this past January. For about two weeks, torrential rains marched in from the Pacific Ocean, killing at least nine people. Rivers breached their banks, waterspouts whirred off the coast and mudslides buried cars. Elsewhere in the state, skiers were delighted: by mid-January parts of the Sierra Nevada had received more than twice their normal snowfall for that part of the season... What's wrong with the weather? What's wrong with it is El Niño.

Adapted from *Earth: The Science of Our Planet*, January 1995

Storm Hazards

Wind damage

Storms such as hurricanes and tornadoes can damage buildings in several ways. High-speed winds can tear off roofs, smash windows or even blow down buildings. In a severe hurricane or tornado, cars, trees, rubbish bins and other debris can be picked up and hurled at buildings. Glass from shattered windows swirls through the air, creating a deadly cloud of sharp fragments.

Severe damage can also be caused as a result of the difference in pressure between the inside of a building and the storm raging outside. In the eye of a hurricane or tornado the air pressure outside can be much lower than the pressure inside, causing many buildings to explode outwards.

▼ A tornado on 4 May 1999 caused this industrial building in Oklahoma, USA, to collapse, damaging the trucks and equipment inside.

Lightning

Lightning occurs when thunderstorms concentrate positive electrical charges in the upper part of cumulonimbus clouds and negative charges in the lower part. When the difference in the charge between the top and bottom of the storm clouds becomes great enough to overcome air resistance, a sudden and violent electrical discharge occurs in the form of a lightning strike or stroke. Although this lasts for only millionths of a second, the temperature of the stroke rises to 28,000 °C, which causes the flash and the thunderclap. Lightning strokes can have four main effects:

- people and animals can be electrocuted
- material in the path of the lightning strike can be vaporized (burnt up)
- the high temperatures of the lightning strike can cause fires
- sudden power surges can damage electrical equipment.

DID YOU KNOW?

Each year in the USA an average of 130 people die as a result of being struck by lightning, while tornadoes kill 125 people and hurricanes 60 people per year.

▼ These diagrams show how lightning occurs.

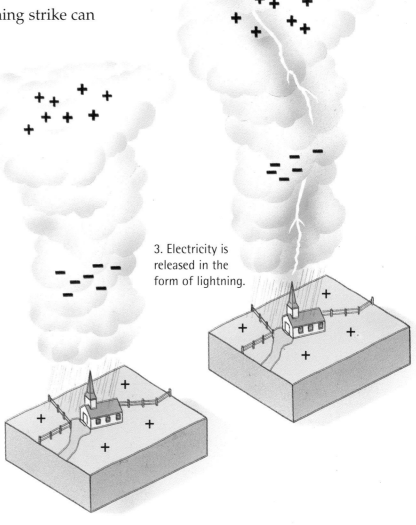

1. Positive electrical charges build up at the top of the cloud.

2. Negative electrical charges build up at the bottom of the cloud. The difference in charge between the top and bottom of the cloud becomes great enough to overcome air resistance.

3. Electricity is released in the form of lightning.

Hail, snow and ice

Few people are killed or injured as a direct result of being caught in a hail or snowstorm. Most people who die in snowstorms are killed in avalanches. However, hail and snowstorms can cause severe damage to crops, trees, powerlines and buildings. In the USA, 2% of the country's crops are destroyed and $760 million-worth of damage is caused by hail and snowstorms every year. Ice-storms caused havoc in eastern Canada in January 1998. As ice formed on power lines, thousands of them were brought down, leaving millions of people without heat in the freezing temperatures.

▼ This traffic light in Montreal, Canada, has been bent over by the weight of the ice that has formed on it.

 DID YOU KNOW?

In 218 BC the north African general Hannibal took 40,000 soldiers across the Alps to invade Rome. Blizzards and avalanches killed 16,000 of his men.

Avalanches

The most devastating after-effects of snowstorms are avalanches. These occur when snow builds up on slopes and then falls without warning. On gentle slopes there is not enough gradient to make the snow fall downhill, and on very steep slopes the snow cannot build up enough to pose a threat. But avalanches are a real danger on slopes that are at an angle of 25°–40°. With up to a million tonnes of snow hurtling down a slope at speeds of over 320 kph, an avalanche can crush everything in its path.

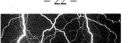

▲ Houses in the small Italian village of Morgex were reduced to rubble by an avalanche on 23 February 1999.

Avalanches are very common – there are about 100,000 each year in the American Rockies alone – but most are in uninhabited areas and are no danger to people. However, as skiing and snowboarding become more popular, more and more people are living, working and spending holidays in areas threatened by avalanches. In the severe snowstorms that hit the Alps in February 1999, 38 people were killed when an avalanche hit the small village of Galtür in Austria.

Deaths in avalanches are caused in three main ways. The first is by the crushing force of the avalanche, especially as the hurtling snow picks up debris, including boulders, rocks and soil, as it falls. Second, people who are buried underneath the snow can quickly suffocate. Those who survive all of this face a third hazard – the intense cold which causes hypothermia and then death.

DID YOU KNOW?

The fastest avalanche ever measured struck at Glarnisch in Switzerland on 6 March 1898. It reached 349 kph and travelled 6.9 km in just over a minute.

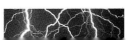

MONSOONS POUR TRAGEDY ON BANGLADESH

Bangladesh's floods are killing people through drowning, electrocution and, most dreaded of all, snake bites. To shop for food, you must wade, or wait for the ferry. To find safe drinking water, you must lug your metal jars hundreds of metres to the nearest hand pump still in use...

In the poor streets of Gulshan, most people have managed to stay on in their homes, building up beds and tables so they are above the water level, though this means living squashed up against the corrugated iron roofs.

Adpated from *The Independent*, 7 September 1998

Floods

Floods can cause billions of pounds-worth of damage and many deaths. In 1998, unusually heavy monsoon rains caused serious flooding in Bangladesh. Floodwater covered over 60% of the country, pouring through the homes and farms of more than 30 million people. The monsoon rains also brought floods to China, and a hurricane made the situation even worse. Many people choose to live on flood plains because the land is good for farming and for building on. But if these areas are hit by unusually stormy weather, the overflowing rivers can bring disaster.

▼ In Bangladesh's capital, Dhaka, people standing waist-high in floodwater queue to collect clean drinking water.

Flash floods sometimes occur when motionless or slow-moving thunderstorms produce heavy rain over a particular area. When this happens, over 50 mm of rain can fall in an hour. The ground very quickly becomes full of water and cannot absorb any more. Water then runs along the surface and into rivers, causing them to overflow.

Melting snow can also cause flash floods, sometimes many hundreds of kilometres from the areas of heavy snowfalls. In February 1999, a sudden thaw followed severe snowstorms in the Alps. Meltwater poured into the rivers and caused serious flooding in parts of Germany and Switzerland. Flash floods are very destructive, not only because there is so little warning of them but also because the water flows so powerfully and contains a lot of mud, sediment and boulders.

Coastal erosion and storm surges

Storms can be a major cause of erosion and flooding around coasts. Heavy rain soaks into the ground and can make cliffs weaker and more likely to collapse. Stronger winds increase the height of the waves pounding the coast line, and these waves can be so high that they form a storm surge. Storm surges can flood the land behind the coast and as the water is sucked back into the sea it erodes the coast.

Some storm surges can be major killers. On 1 February 1953 a North Sea storm surge hit eastern Britain and the Netherlands, damaging 400,000 buildings, and killing 1,835 people and 47,000 cattle.

▲ Storm waves batter the rocky coastline of northern France.

 DID YOU KNOW?
The cliffs at Beachy Head in Sussex, England, are a famous landmark. In January 1999, a combination of erosion by the sea and three weeks of heavy rain caused a spectacular rock fall. Around 50,000 tonnes of rock crashed from the cliffs in a single day.

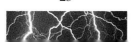

Predicting Storms

Scientists know that certain types of storm tend to develop in certain climate areas (see pages 8–19). The climate of an area is the general pattern of weather that occurs over a period of at least thirty years. But to predict when a storm is going to develop, scientists need to understand how the weather changes from day to day.

Measuring the weather

Satellites, ground weather stations, and weather ships, balloons and aircraft are all used to collect weather data. Meteorologists use this information to map changes in temperature, atmospheric pressure and cloud cover.
This helps them to predict what will happen to the weather over the next few days.

◀ This is a geostationary weather satellite (see page 28) which is monitoring weather patterns over Europe and Africa.

Chaos Theory

Predicting the weather is very difficult. Think of all those times when the weather report on television says it will be sunny and it rains instead. There are, however, reasons why weather is so unpredictable and this is explained by the Chaos Theory. Scientists now know that very small changes in the temperature, pressure and humidity of the atmosphere can have unpredictable or 'chaotic' effects on large-scale weather patterns, for example by altering the strength and direction of a hurricane. This is also called the Butterfly Effect, because changes in weather conditions that seem no more significant than the flapping of a butterfly's wings can occasionally have a major effect on the weather.

▲ This automatic weather station has instruments for measuring wind speed and direction (top left), temperature, humidity and the intensity of sunlight. The meteorologist is transferring the data recorded by the weather station to his own computer.

Meteorologists never know which of the small weather changes will combine to produce a major effect. They can predict general patterns in the weather – for example, they can say that May is the worst month for tornadoes in the USA. But they cannot predict exactly when or where a tornado will occur. Even with the help of powerful computers and detailed weather maps provided by satellites, meteorologists cannot accurately forecast the weather more than two days ahead.

◀ This weather balloon measures humidity, temperature and wind speeds.

Predicting hurricanes

Weather satellites are the most important instruments for detecting and tracking hurricanes. Two types of satellite are used: polar orbiting satellites, which spin around the Earth from Pole to Pole, and geostationary satellites, which remain in the same position above the Earth all the time. These satellites can detect clusters of rain clouds and track them to see if they develop into a hurricane.

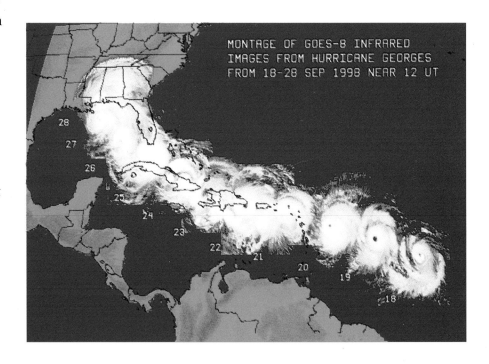

MONTAGE OF GOES-8 INFRARED IMAGES FROM HURRICANE GEORGES FROM 18-28 SEP 1998 NEAR 12 UT

Predicting landfall

If a hurricane does develop, it is vital to be able to predict when and where it will reach land, or 'make landfall', so that people living in the danger zone can be evacuated. For 70 per cent of hurricanes, forecasters can predict the paths they will take up to 24 hours in advance, using information about their direction and speed over the previous 36 hours. A combination of very detailed climate data and large computer models can be used for hurricanes whose path is more difficult to predict. However, even the complex computer models do not always get it right; the disaster caused by Hurricane Mitch is an example of what happens when the predictions are wrong (see pages 32–5).

▲ This computer image shows the path taken by Hurricane Georges across the Caribbean Sea and southern states of the USA from 18–28 September 1998.

A 3-D computer image of a hurricane, ▶ created using satellite data. It shows Hurricane Linda off the coast of Mexico in 1997. The hole in the centre is the 'eye' of the storm, an area of calm air and very low pressure.

Hurricane warnings

Even with the help of satellite tracking and computer models, forecasters know that a hurricane may change course at the last moment. This is why they usually issue hurricane warnings just 12–18 hours before they expect the hurricane to make landfall.

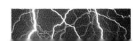

Famous Storms

'The prepared' – Hurricane Gilbert, 1988

Hurricane Gilbert hit the Caribbean island of Jamaica on 12 September 1988. It was one of the worst storms ever recorded in the Caribbean. The eye of the storm was over 40 km in diameter, with wind speeds of 150 kph and gusts reaching 225 kph. After striking Jamaica, the hurricane moved on to Mexico, where 200 people were killed. In Texas, USA, weather conditions linked to the storm triggered 40 tornadoes and caused $10 billion-worth of damage.

Since Jamaica is frequently in the path of hurricanes, a lot of work had been done to produce evacuation and shelter plans. These were very successful. Although 45 people died, 11 of these were shot by the police for looting shops while everyone else was sheltering from the storm. The real problem the island faced, however, was the effect on its economy. Losses reached $3,000 million, which is about the same amount of money as the whole island earns in a year. The impact that Hurricane Gilbert had on Jamaica shows that, however much planning is done in advance, nothing can prevent a really severe storm from causing serious damage.

▲ This house in Jamaica has been hit by a falling tree. Many houses were badly damaged by the high winds of Hurricane Gilbert.

▼ This map shows the path of Hurricane Gilbert across the Caribbean and southern USA.

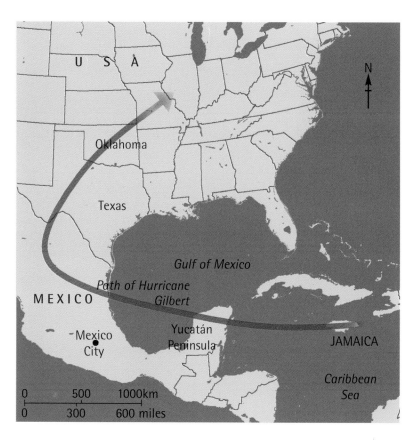

The damage

One in four houses in Jamaica were damaged, usually by having their roofs ripped off. In one case the roof was ripped off a church in which 400 people were sheltering. Some types of building were affected more badly than others. For example, more than 500 of the 580 schools on the island were damaged. Ten of Jamaica's hospitals were damaged, just at the time when they were most needed. When the roof was blown off the country's main telephone exchange, rain destroyed the switchboard, cutting all telephone lines. Radio and television masts were brought down by the winds. The lack of communications prevented the authorities from organizing an efficient rescue effort. There was a lot of damage to crops and industry, although fortunately over 40 per cent of businesses were insured.

Lessons learnt

Before Hurricane Gilbert, many roofs were made from aluminium sheeting which is very cheap in Jamaica. But strong winds can easily tear this metal away from its fasteners. The law in Jamaica has now been changed to try to reduce this problem. All new buildings must be able to survive a three-second gust of 200 kph without suffering serious damage.

▲ Hurricane Gilbert caused chaos throughout the Caribbean. This ship was washed ashore in Mexico.

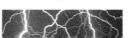

'The unprepared' – Hurricane Mitch, 1998

On 28 October 1998, Hurricane Mitch hit Central America. It was the most destructive hurricane in 200 years, with sustained wind speeds of 290 kph and 60 cm of rain falling each day. There were two killer blows – the destruction caused by the high winds and the massive floods which followed the torrential rain. The people of the region were totally unprepared for the disaster. We will never know how many people were killed, as many of the bodies are still buried under metres of mud brought down by the floods. However, estimates suggest that over 20,000 were killed and up to two million made homeless.

 EYEWITNESS

"I have seen earthquakes, droughts, two wars, cyclones and tidal waves. But this is undoubtedly the worst thing I have ever seen."

Cardinal Miguel Obando y Bravo of Managua, Nicaragua, quoted in *The Independent*, 4 November 1998.

▼ People from the town of El Progreso in Honduras struggle to reach their homes and look for their possessions.

HURRICANE EXPERTS ADMIT THEY FAILED

Jerry Jarrell, director of the National Hurricane Centre in Miami, USA, admitted that the traditional method of forecasting hurricanes – using a five-point scale to measure wind speed – had proved woefully inadequate this year. `This scale was designed to give a visual picture of winds. It doesn't talk about rainfall,' Mr Jarrell said.

He suggested a study into a new system that would predict how much rain a hurricane would carry. Mr Jarrell also implied that communications problems in poorer regions may have played a part in the disaster. `In the initial warning we put out we had a problem contacting Honduras,' he said.

Adapted from *The Independent*, 2 December 1998

▼ This map shows how Central America was affected by Hurricane Mitch.

The National Hurricane Center and the Hurricane Research Center, both in Miami in the USA, admit that they got the prediction of Hurricane Mitch wrong. The computer models predicted that when the storm was in the Caribbean Sea it would turn west. Instead, it turned south and crashed into the poorest countries of Central America. The scientists believe that they had not taken account of the strength of El Niño (see pages 18–19), which may have helped to drag Hurricane Mitch across Central America into the Pacific Ocean.

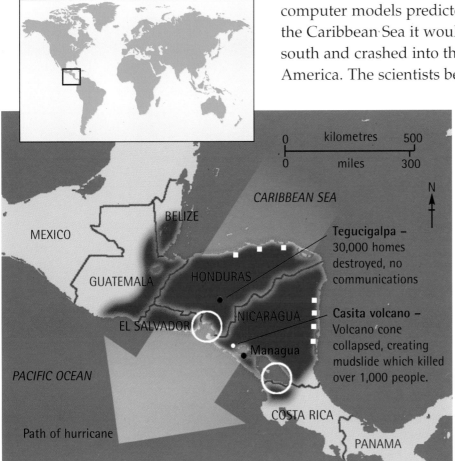

Tegucigalpa – 30,000 homes destroyed, no communications

Casita volcano – Volcano cone collapsed, creating mudslide which killed over 1,000 people.

Path of hurricane

Key

☐ Towns and villages cut off

○ Very severe floods

■ Farmland destroyed

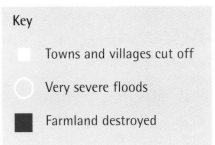

The damage

The worst-hit country was Honduras, which has a population of nearly 6 million. Flooding was so severe that 85 per cent of the country was under water. For example, for ten days after the rains of Hurricane Mitch, the Hamuya River, which is usually a quiet, calm stretch of water about 60 m wide, became a roaring torrent 500 m wide. Over 100 bridges, 80 per cent of the roads and 75 per cent of the country's agriculture were destroyed. Most of the banana plantations were lost. It is estimated that the total repair bill for all the damage done by Hurricane Mitch will be over $2 billion.

▼ Laura Arriola de Guity is hurried away on a stretcher, following her dramatic rescue. A helicopter crew had spotted her floating far out at sea.

Lessons learnt

The inadequate warning of the hurricane did contribute to the devastation in Central America. However, the most important lesson of Hurricane Mitch is that extremely poor countries just do not have the money and infrastructure to deal with the damage that can be caused by natural disasters. The Nicaraguan government, for example, struggled to find enough money to fuel their ageing helicopters, which were needed to deliver aid and rescue people caught by the floods.

66 EYEWITNESS 99

"I swam and swam, trying to save my son, trying to get somewhere dry. And then I realized I was already in the sea. I was begging God to let someone find me and rescue me. But there was no one. No one saw me. The worst part for me was after being with my whole family, with my children, my husband, that I could be so alone in the sea without seeing anybody."

Laura Arriola de Guity, who was swept out to sea by the floods that hit Honduras and found six days later, 120 km from her home. Her whole family was killed.

The other major lesson of Hurricane Mitch is that the international relief organizations and foreign governments must respond faster when disaster strikes. Hurricane Mitch destroyed transport and communications, leaving hundreds of communities cut off from the outside world. Without food supplies and medical help, starvation and disease became widespread. It took weeks to work out what help was needed and for aid to be distributed. The countries affected are so poor that they could not pay for the relief work themselves. The international community has provided help worth $100 million. Yet this is a drop in the ocean compared to the $5 billion that could be needed to rebuild Central America.

▲ These houses in Honduras' capital city, Tegucigalpa, were destroyed by a mudslide on 3 November, 1998. The mudslide was caused by the heavy rains of Hurricane Mitch.

Tornado Alley, USA

Tornado Alley stretches across the Midwest of the USA, centred on Kansas and Oklahoma. Here, the warm air from the Gulf of Mexico meets cold, dry air from the north. This creates perfect conditions for towering thunderclouds to form, and these can unleash devastating tornadoes.

Oklahoma, 1999

On 4 May 1999 the fiercest tornadoes to hit the USA for ten years struck the states of Kansas and Oklahoma. Approximately 40 separate tornadoes touched down, killing at least 43 people and injuring 700 others. One of the tornadoes that hit Oklahoma City caused wind speeds of 511 kph, the fastest ever recorded. The force of the winds was so great that paving stones were ripped up and hurled around. Oklahoma City alone suffered £800 million-worth of damage.

DID YOU KNOW?
The Tri-State tornado raced across Missouri, Illinois and Indiana, USA, at speeds of over 80 kph on 18 March 1925. It killed 695 people and is the most destructive tornado ever recorded.

▼ A teenager searches through the wreckage of his home after it was destroyed by a tornado in May 1999.

'Terrible Tuesday'

The worst outbreak of tornadoes in the USA took place on 3 April 1974. This day became known as `Terrible Tuesday'. An incredible 148 tornadoes touched down in twelve states from Michigan to Alabama. At least 300 people were killed and over 5,000 injured.

Chasing tornadoes

The National Severe Storms Laboratory in Norman, Oklahoma, is right in the centre of Tornado Alley. Scientists set out from here to chase tornadoes as they develop, trying to learn more about these destructive storms. They know what kind of weather conditions cause tornadoes to form. What they have not yet learnt is how to tell whether a particularly severe thunderstorm will produce a tornado. When they find the answer to this question, they will be able to issue more accurate warnings, and there will be much less chance of a tornado catching people unprepared.

▲ Dramatic shots like this one, of a tornado in the US Midwest, are taken by 'tornado chasers', who enjoy the thrill of getting close to the violent storm.

66 EYEWITNESS 99

"I was working that day as a forecaster for the National Weather Service in Louisville, Kentucky. About half an hour after the tornado warning was issued, we saw a thunderstorm approaching. As the cloud moved overhead we could see the funnel cloud forming. Suddenly, an instrument shelter which was bolted to a rooftop deck collapsed in front of our window. The tornado had reached the roof without a visible funnel.

This tornado was one of 148 twisters recorded during the outbreak. For me, it was the most spectacular, as it was the first tornado I witnessed."

John Forsing recalls his experiences on Terrible Tuesday, 3 April 1974 (adapted from a report by the National Oceanographic and Atmospheric Administration, USA).

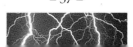

Alpine snowstorms, 1999

❝ EYEWITNESS ❞

"We were drinking hot, mulled wine when suddenly it started. The lights went out. It was dark. There was only dust and snow. We got out of there as fast as we could."

Franz Wekno, hotel owner, Galtür, Austria.

In February 1999 the European Alps were hit by a massive series of snowstorms and suffered the heaviest snowfalls in living memory. The storms cut road and rail links, isolating ski resorts throughout the central and western Alps and leaving tens of thousands of tourists stranded. The snowfall was so heavy and sudden that many avalanches were set off, killing over 70 people.

Avalanche in Austria

The worst avalanches struck the villages of Galtür and Valzur in the Paznaun valley, south-west of Innsbruck in Austria. The avalanches were the first in the area for many years and the villages were not protected by avalanche barriers. Thirty-eight people were killed.

▼ Rescuers dig into the deep snow as they search for victims of the avalanche in Galtür, Austria.

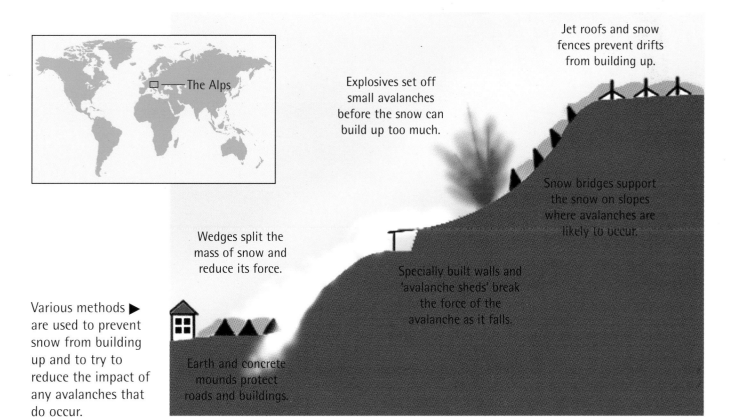

Explosives set off small avalanches before the snow can build up too much.

Jet roofs and snow fences prevent drifts from building up.

Snow bridges support the snow on slopes where avalanches are likely to occur.

Wedges split the mass of snow and reduce its force.

Specially built walls and 'avalanche sheds' break the force of the avalanche as it falls.

Earth and concrete mounds protect roads and buildings.

Various methods ▶ are used to prevent snow from building up and to try to reduce the impact of any avalanches that do occur.

RESCUE FATALLY DELAYED

Left to their own devices, holidaymakers and locals grabbed torches and organized rescue parties. First-aid boxes in cars that could be reached were raided. Unfortunately, emergency equipment had been stored at the fire station, which had lain directly in the path of the avalanche. In the few hours when it really mattered, the lifesaving tools were buried under tonnes of snow.

Adapted from *The Independent on Sunday*, 28 February 1999

The snow-drifts were so deep that the only way to get in and out of the Paznaun valley was by helicopter. The terrible weather prevented the specialist rescue squads from getting to the area until 16 hours after the avalanche. When the rescue squads arrived they found the villagers had spent the night frantically digging with their bare hands to find people buried below tonnes of snow.

Lessons learnt

Usually avalanches can be controlled by setting up barriers and using explosives to set off small avalanches before the snow can build up too much. This technique is used at all ski resorts and in other high-risk areas. However, on this occasion the snowfall was extremely sudden and heavy in areas that are not usually at risk from avalanches, so little could be done in advance to prevent the disaster. The number of people killed was only a small percentage of those in the area at the time, which shows that people living and holidaying in the Alps are generally well-protected.

Rescue and Prevention

Rescue and relief plans

Storms and other natural disasters will always occur. With more research, scientists will be better able to predict when and where 'killer' storms will hit. However, governments and rescue agencies know that they must plan for the worst.

Once a storm has hit, local authorities urgently need to organize the rescue of people who are trapped. People buried in avalanches, for example, can die within 30 minutes if they are not found. If a building collapses in a hurricane or tornado, fewer than half the people trapped under the rubble are likely to be alive in six hours' time. Rescuers use a system called 'triage' to decide which casualties are to be treated first. Those who are very severely injured and likely to die, together with people who have only minor injuries, are left untreated. Rescuers concentrate their efforts on those who have a reasonable chance of survival if they are given basic medical help.

The major problem with storm disasters is that rescue and relief efforts usually have to begin while the effects of the storm are still being felt. For example, during the 1999 snowstorms in the Alps the snow was so heavy that all roads were closed for days and for much of the time the weather was too bad to use helicopters.

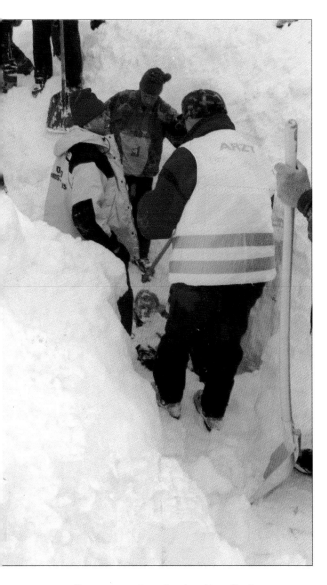

▲ Rescue workers in the Alps find a person trapped under the snow.

 EYEWITNESS

"We could have started the airlift 30 minutes after the avalanche, but the best plans amount to nothing in bad weather."

Wendelin Weingartner, governor of Tyrol province, Austria, January 1999

Relief and Rescue Plan

1. Assess overall damage

2. Immediate rescue of trapped people

3. Provide medical assistance from outside the area

4. Assess human need for food, water and shelter

5. Distribute emergency aid

6. Assess condition of buildings and bridges, pull down dangerous structures

7. Restore communications and start up businesses again

8. Begin rebuilding using storm-resistant material

9. Start programme of storm education

Disease

One of the biggest problems after any major natural disaster is the spread of disease. Many of the worst diseases take four to five days to develop, and if not controlled can kill as many people as the storm itself. Disease was a particularly severe problem after Hurricane Mitch. With so many dead bodies not buried, so much stagnant water from the flood, and people stranded without access to clean water and medicines, diseases such as cholera were able to spread rapidly.

Mitigation and education

Efforts to reduce the damage caused by storms are called mitigation. Point nine on the 'Rescue and Relief Plan' (left) is to start a programme of storm education. The authorities assess the damage a storm is likely to cause and make plans to minimize it. For example, existing buildings might have to be strengthened and stricter laws brought in on how buildings should be constructed. Storm education also involves developing evacuation procedures and educating people about how to react if a storm threatens.

Reducing poverty

It is much harder for poor countries to cope with the after-effects of storms. In Nicaragua, for example, only 58 per cent of the population had access to fresh water *before* Hurricane Mitch struck. After the disaster, the situation was much worse. More than a third of the population is unable to read or write, making it difficult to develop effective storm education plans. The countries of Central America owe millions of dollars to wealthier countries – Nicaragua has debts of almost $6,000 million. Following Hurricane Mitch, many people called for these international debts to be cancelled, so that the countries of Central America could afford to repair the damage caused by the storm.

◀ A relief and rescue plan should include the following stages.

The Future

Global warming

Carbon dioxide and water vapour in the atmosphere produce a natural 'greenhouse effect', raising the temperature of the Earth's surface and making it warm enough for life to exist. However, over the last 150 years industries have been pumping increasing amounts of gases such as carbon dioxide, methane and nitrous oxides into the atmosphere. As the level of carbon dioxide in the atmosphere has risen, temperatures on Earth have increased. This is known as global warming.

Stronger storms

Evidence suggests that global warming may be making storms stronger and more frequent. For example, there is a strong relationship between the surface temperature of the seas and the number of hurricanes that occur. In 1995 the surface of the Atlantic Ocean was exceptionally hot and this coincided with an amazing eleven hurricanes and nineteen tropical storms, double the annual average over the previous fifty years.

▲ A new office block mangled by the freak hurricane that hit Britain in 1987. Global warming may increase the risk of unusual weather events like this.

HURRICANE KILLS SIX IN MOSCOW

At least six people died during a sudden, violent storm on Saturday night in Moscow. The Russian media were describing the storm as an *uragan*, or hurricane. The gale occurred after two weeks of unusually hot weather that has sent temperatures soaring well above 30 °C and set off scores of forest fires. Storms are rare in Moscow and the mayor has criticized forecasters for failing to warn citizens about the *uragan* – another freak weather phenomenon in a strange year.

Adapted from *The Guardian*, 22 September 1998

Global warming is likely to make weather features such as storms behave in ways that are actually more difficult to predict. For the millions of people living in the monsoon zone, for example, this is a very serious issue. They rely on the regular monsoon rains to provide life-giving water. If the difference in temperatures between the northern and southern hemispheres changes even slightly, it can affect the direction and intensity of the monsoons, leading to droughts in some areas and terrible floods in others.

DID YOU KNOW?
Average annual temperatures have been rising steadily since 1980, and 1997 and 1998 were the two hottest years on record.

▼ These floods in China in 1998 followed an unusually heavy monsoon. The floods killed 3,700 people and caused £19 billion-worth of damage.

El Niño and global warming

El Niño (see pages 18–19) usually occurs every three to seven years. Since 1991, it has returned in 1991–2, 1992–3, 1994–5 and 1997–8. Some scientists believe that El Niño is returning more often and having more damaging effects because of global warming.

By studying the growth patterns of corals in the Pacific Ocean, scientists have been able to work out what the surface temperatures of the ocean have been over the last 200 years. This data shows that for much of that time, El Niño returned, on average, every five years. Over the last forty years, El Niño has been occurring, on average, more than once every three years. But La Niña – the period when the ocean becomes cooler than normal – has been occurring less frequently. One explanation for this may be that global warming is making the oceans warmer, and so the climatic conditions which produce El Niño are occurring more often.

◀ A rain forest burns in the very dry conditions that affected Brazil in 1998. The usual seasonal rains did not arrive, probably as a result of El Niño.

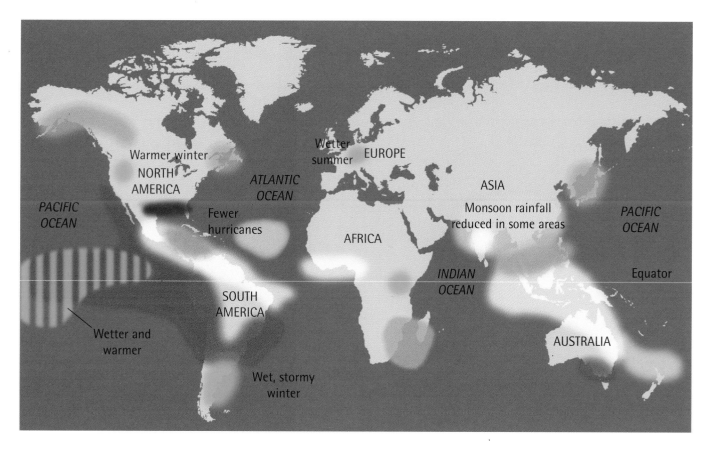

Warmer winter
NORTH
AMERICA

Wetter
summer   EUROPE

ATLANTIC
OCEAN

ASIA

PACIFIC
OCEAN

Fewer
hurricanes

Monsoon rainfall
reduced in some areas

PACIFIC
OCEAN

AFRICA

SOUTH
AMERICA

INDIAN
OCEAN

Equator

Wetter and
warmer

AUSTRALIA

Wet, stormy
winter

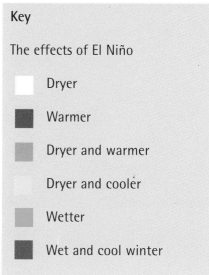

Key

The effects of El Niño

Dryer

Warmer

Dryer and warmer

Dryer and cooler

Wetter

Wet and cool winter

▲ This map shows the areas of the world that experienced changes in their usual climate during 1998. Many scientists believe these changes were the result of El Niño.

The 1997–98 El Niño was the strongest on record. Droughts in the southern USA, East Africa, northern India, north-east Brazil and Australia were all linked to El Niño. In Indonesia, forest fires burned out of control in the very dry conditions, producing a thick, choking smog which spread into neighbouring countries. In California, parts of South America, the Pacific, Sri Lanka and east central Africa there were torrential rains.

Will a combination of El Niño and global warming lead to a stormier future? Scientists cannot yet tell for certain, but they know that storms are already the most threatening natural destructive forces on the planet. Hurricanes alone cause more damage and loss of life per year than earthquakes. This is why it is so vital for scientists to find out more about how these powerful forces will affect our daily lives in the future.

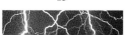

Glossary

Atmospheric pressure The amount of air that is pressing down on the Earth. When there is high pressure a lot of air is pressing down; when there is low pressure less air is pressing down.

Avalanche The rapid movement of large quantities of snow, ice, mud and rocks down a steep slope.

Blizzard A severe winter storm with strong winds, ice, hail and driving snow.

Cirrus cloud High, white cloud that forms in long, wispy strands.

Climate The general weather conditions in different areas of the world. Climate is sometimes described as the average weather over a period of 30 years.

Coriolis force The way in which air and ocean currents are pushed eastwards or westwards as a result of the spin of the Earth on its axis.

Cumulonimbus cloud Very large, thick clouds which tower to a great height. They look dark at the base because they are so thick.

El Niño This is a change in the atmospheric pressure over the Pacific which leads to weaker Trade winds and enables currents of warm water to flow towards South America.

Equator An imaginary line that runs around the middle of the Earth, halfway between the North and South Poles.

Erosion The removal of rocks and soil by the action of wind and water.

Fujita Tornado Intensity Scale A system of classifying tornadoes on a seven-point scale (F0–F6), according to the speed of their winds and the damage they are likely to cause.

Hemisphere Half of the Earth. The Equator divides the Earth into the northern and southern hemispheres.

Humidity The amount of water vapour that is in the air.

Hurricane A swirling storm in which wind speeds are above 120 kph.

Hypothermia Very low body temperatures caused by intense cold. People suffering hypothermia can die very quickly.

Infrastructure The transport, communications and government organizations that allow a country to function efficiently.

International aid Money provided by many different countries to help other countries cope with disasters such as storms.

Jet stream A narrow belt of strong winds blowing at speeds of 160–320 kph, at a height of 9–14 km above the Earth. Jet streams form at the Polar Front and the Subtropical Highs.

Latitude A way of describing the distance of a particular point from the Equator, measured as an angle from the Equator.

Meteorologist A scientist who studies the atmosphere in order to predict the weather.

Monsoon The heavy rains that occur at particular times of year in southern Asia and central Africa.

Pearson Scale A system of classifying tornadoes, according to the length and width of their path.

Relief organizations Groups that provide money, food, shelter, equipment and people with special skills, such as doctors, to help countries deal with disasters.

Tornado A violent, spinning column of air.

Trade winds The winds that blow either side of the Equator, from the north-east in the northern hemisphere and the south-east in the southern hemisphere.

Tropics The hot regions of the Earth that span the Equator from 30 $^{\circ}$N to 30 $^{\circ}$S.

Water vapour Water which is in the air in the form of a gas. It is released as rain or snow when the air cools.

Further Information

BOOKS AND ARTICLES

Air (Against the Elements series) by S. Angliss (Watts, 1998)
A Closer Look at Hurricanes and Typhoons by J. Green (Watts, 1996)
The Complete Book of the Earth by A. Claybourne, G. Doherty and R. Treays (Usborne, 1999)
Hurricanes and Storms by Nicola Barber (Evans, 1993)
The Kingfisher Book of Planet Earth by Martin Redfern (Kingfisher, 1999)
Restless Planet: Floods by Dr Mark Maslin (Wayland, 1999)

CD-ROMS

Violent Earth (Wayland Multimedia, 1997) PC and MAC versions available. Looks at floods, hurricanes, tornadoes and duststorms, plus earthquakes and volcanoes.

WEBSITES

The World Wide Web has hundreds of sites providing information about storms. Here are a few places to start.

http://www.bgs.ac.uk/bgs/w3/beachy/beachy.htm
This website provides information and superb pictures of the Beachy Head cliff collapse.

http://www.geocities.com/Vienna/3885/storm.htm
Try this web site to find out more about tornadoes.

http://www.geog.ucl.ac.uk/ecrc
This is the website for the Environmental Change Research Centre at University College London. You could also try the Benfield Greig Hazard Research Centre at:
http://www.ucl.ac.uk/geolsci/research/ben-grei/

http://hurricane.terrapin.com/en/
Details of hurricanes and storms being tracked in the Atlantic and Pacific Oceans are on this web site.

http://www.osei.noaa.gov/OSEIstormind.html
This website provides the latest news on storms from around the world.

http://www.pmel.noaa.gov/toga-tao/el-nino/home.html
Try this website for more information about El Niño.

http://www.storms97.com
http://www.tiac.net/users/bernardo/wx/hurricane.html
Further information about hurricanes is available on these sites.

Index

Page numbers in bold refer to illustrations.